Listening for Grace Notes

Listening for Grace Notes

Poems by

Alida Woods

© 2025 Alida Woods. All rights reserved.
This material may not be reproduced in any form, published,
reprinted, recorded, performed, broadcast,
rewritten, or redistributed without
the explicit permission of Alida Woods.
All such actions are strictly prohibited by law.

Cover design by Shay Culligan
Cover art by Brigitte Knauf, Asheville, NC.
Proceeds from Knauf's art support World Central Kitchen,
Doctors Without Borders, and Helene Relief Fund.
Author photo by Geordie Woods, Sight Savers International, UK.

ISBN: 978-1-63980-735-2

Kelsay Books
502 South 1040 East, A-119
American Fork, Utah 84003
Kelsaybooks.com

in memory of my mother

&

for my children and grandchildren

Acknowledgments

My thanks to the editors of the journals where the following poems have appeared:

Artemis: "Susan B. Anthony and the Tooth Fairy" published as "Dear Tooth Fairy," "In Search of the Blue Throated Motmot"
Great Smokies Review: "Morning with Onion," "What She Carried," "Smallness and Wonder" published as "My Smallness Leaves Space for Wonder," "The Weight of Socks," "A Vacancy"
Litmosphere: "Forgetting"
Smokey Blue Literary Arts Magazine: "Waking," "Ghost Daughters" published as "Selena"

Contents

How to Shuck an Oyster	13
Smallness and Wonder	15
A Ghazal of Birds	16
The Angle of Refraction	17
Some Things to Know About Birders	18
In Search of the Blue Throated Motmot	20
Turkey Vultures	21
Monster Poppies	22
August	23
A Legacy of Oars	24
The Weight of Socks	25
Susan B. Anthony and the Tooth Fairy	26
The Sleep of Warriors	27
Incongruence	28
The Weight of Words	29
Morning with Onion	30
The Sound of Sleep	32
Forgetting	33
Photo of My Parents in Their Kitchen	35
What She Carried	37
Peaches and Ghosts	39
We are ghost daughters	40
A Vacancy	41
darkening	42
Sunset on the Edisto River	43
Waking	44
Gladiolas	46
Pomme	48
Mums	49
Nothing to a Mountain	51

*I pray to the birds because they remind me
of what I love rather than what I fear.
At the end of my prayers they teach me to listen.*

—Terry Tempest Williams

How to Shuck an Oyster

for Ali, Samish Bay Washington

Begin with the towel
folded and layered to protect you
as you cut into the shell.

Lay it like a prayer cloth
for the sacrament
you are about to perform. Anticipate

the brine. Hold the shucking knife
tight, tap the oyster to be sure it's alive,
wrap the oyster hinge end out.

Hold it firmly in the towel,
enter through the hinge,
twist to open the nacreous chamber.

Slide the knife along the jagged edge,
cradling the bivalve as you would
unburied treasure. Feel the depth of your hunger.

Go slow, notice everything—the salt on your lip,
the smell of the ocean in your hand.
Be patient—reward is slow to reveal itself.

Keep your intent clear
as you release the muscle gripping
the upper shell. Do not be distracted

by the gulls on the bay
calling you to another
time and place.

Listen as the waves lap
the pebbled shore and you lay
the open shell on ice.

Smallness and Wonder

The small self is probably one of the defining elements of awe.
—Dacher Keltner

You think you're so big is what we said as we marshalled
our 11-year-old selves into
the pre-adolescent pecking order. The world was big.
None of us felt big enough.

The world
is still big and I am big enough
to be small.

My eye to the elephant's glassy brown orb,
a watery portal to this 6,000-pound mystery.
Her patient stare holds
me in an immensity, gathers up my smallness.

Pungent sage hovers in the still noon.
I stand in the Valley of Fire reading
the colossal rock, the sepia stories of hunting and gathering
as this minute fades
into millennia. My story is small.

The Zambezi thunders over the edge of the earth, spray catching
the full moonlight. A rainbow reaches over us
across the divide so loud
we cannot hear each other's awe.

My husband tells me the warblers have arrived.
They are here, he tells me,
feeding for nocturnal flight from as far away as Patagonia,
their flight sometimes 40,000 feet
above the trees. We look up at the stars guiding them north,
my smallness next to his.

A Ghazal of Birds

In the tool shed a wren builds a nest under the eaves.
Dry winter grasses cradle three tiny eggs, she leaves.

This morning a chorus of robins breaks over the cove.
They welcome day even before night leaves.

I gather my garden tools, I am eye-to-eye with
mother wren. She has returned and I must leave.

Today a caravan of people at the border waits for entry
from a country they must leave.

Each day we watch from the porch with binoculars
and wonder at her patience, hoping she will not leave.

Children taken to strange cities wonder
why they are here and why their mothers leave.

Wrens mate for life. The father carries food and bedding
for the nest. The mother never leaves.

Wrens have over thirty-two songs. How many songs
are remembered by a child whose mother leaves?

Whee-ul-dee-dee, come to me. It will be days before they fledge.
We wait, we trust, we believe.

In the woods behind my house a tangle of birdsong,
these birds are migrants, passing through, they will leave.

The Angle of Refraction

The osprey rises from the tangle,
pockets air under her wings
and plunges, feet first into the fish-rippled
river. Her eyes correct for the catch.

I've spent my life correcting for the catch:
teacher, not anthropologist,
two husbands, not one perfect man,
home in the mountains, not by the sea.

My mother, blind at 80, corrected her life daily.
In December my husband spotted a woodpecker
in the elm outside her window, *Downy,* he pronounced.
That's a hairy, she corrected.

Now when birds return in June
she hears the phoebes
in the meadow
where she can no longer walk.

When I was 19, sure I'd lose my virginity to the man
I would marry, I found myself on a hilltop
overlooking Florence, in love with the adventure of love.
That's when I believed I would be young forever.

The osprey hoists herself,
wings spanning the horizon,
she wrests her rainbow catch
and oars her way over the darkened pines.

Some Things to Know About Birders

Mostly, they are introverts,
geeks and wonks
who enjoy the chase
      and a good Scotch at the end of the day, mostly
      in the company of birders.

Mostly, they are hopeful,
even in the vanishing of feathers,
the thinning of wings.
      Three billion gone since 1970,
      that's 28% in fifty years.

Mostly, they are amateurs,
and require little equipment,
although, it's true,
      the cost of some binoculars
      could fund a small Caribbean island.

According to The U.S. Fish and Wildlife Service,
mostly they are white.
      The list is long: Mick Jagger, Jimmy Carter,
      Agatha Christie, my mechanic, and the seven-year-old
      homeschooler I met in Jackson Park.

Two important rules for Birding While Black—
Always carry your binoculars, Never bird while wearing a hoodie.
#BlackBirdersWeek took place May 31, 2020,
      six days after the murder of George Floyd
      and the day Christian Cooper spotted
      a Kirkland Warbler in Central Park.

Mostly, they are passionate,
driven to extremes of patience.
    My husband waited twelve hours
    in the Guatemalan rainforest
    for a fleeting glimpse of the blue throated motmot.

Mostly, I hope they are like my neighbor, Bill,
for whom every day is Sunday—
coffee cup and binoculars on the porch
    and, like my grandsons, who at two,
    know the way the cardinal sings.

In Search of the Blue Throated Motmot

*Ecosystems are not more complex than we think,
they are more complex than we can think.*
—Frank Egler

After twelve hours in a Guatemalan rainforest
my patience is spent, but you
catch every twitch of branch

each quiver of leaf
until he's there in the circle of your spotter-scope.
Believing is seeing.

At home you explain the warblers
are passing through & that patience is not virtue
but born of passion as we listen

in the soundlessness just before a storm.
Your stillness astounds me as you sit catching birdsong
like grace-notes. What seems like doing nothing is doing

everything. Below, the ferns you planted,
hay-scented and maiden-hair, tangle with invading
honeysuckle, none strives for prominence & like you

I believe that seeing is a form of worship,
hearing as you do,
the wood thrush at the end of the day.

Turkey Vultures

Like old women
they glide
into place
on the arms and elbows
of lifeless oaks.
At the edge of the wood
a cloud of wings
blankets the sky.
What am I to tell
my three-year old grandson
who believes they are dragons?

Monster Poppies

In May they lift their torches
in the garden-gone-to-seed
down the street. I covet
their perfect blooms, delicate
as my grandmother's demitasse.
These splendid orange cups wave
high above the phlox and primrose.

In August crepe-like petals fall
like tired party favors.
I snatch a handful
of the tightly sealed pods,
and hoard them
in my stash of stolen seeds.

But in my garden, they daunt
well-behaved coreopsis and peony.
Over six feet tall they are freaks
mouthing off at the sky,
interlopers, who mock me—
my lust for the exotic,
my pretense of order,
outsmarted by roots and rhizomes.

What is it, I wonder,
about a garden
that is at once
therapist and gallery?

August

Summer spreads like honey
      thick and golden
      into coves   down alleyways.

      Leaves linger
           Fall   yellow
               in drifts   on sidewalks.

A thousand wings hum
      into the slow
      heat of afternoon

      sluggish days
           dwindle into
           darker dusks.

Night comes sooner
      folds abandoned gardens
      like well-read letters.

      A single firefly
           dips furtive
           above the darkened tree-line.

Stillness settles in the wood
         where trees bend
         like prayers

as we listen for grace
      notes in the hollows
      of our bones.

A Legacy of Oars

The blue dinghy rights itself at river's edge
as my father pulls the long oak poles over the gunnels,
gathers up bucket, sponge, oarlocks,
and checks that ropes are taut,
sails stuffed in the stiff canvas sack.

We make our way to the boathouse,
squishing soft sedges underfoot.
My children, 5 and 8, lift their feet to navigate
this tickle of marsh. Each struggles to carry
an oar, their bright orange life jackets dangling
from freckled shoulders. They deposit gear
on rusted hooks between spider webs
and soggy boat cushions.

These rituals of detail—
splendid with salt, the river's journey,
all this greenness tucked deep in memory
as the horizon opens before us, grey in fading light.
The dinghy bobs patiently at the mooring.

The Weight of Socks

The basket of wet laundry feels like lead—
the wicker creaks between us
as we carry it together from the house
to the line behind the shed. Dewy grass
is cold on my bare feet, the toes of her
sneakers—dark with damp. We pause,
unravel sheets braided and askew. She
takes an edge where our hands meet.
We fold them lengthwise in half and clip
the corners to the line leaving clothespins
black with mildew at the bottom of the sack.
Sheets sweat, flapping in the humid air.
We untangle socks and hang them
one by one with almost unbearable care.

Susan B. Anthony and the Tooth Fairy

From under freshly fluffed pillows
I extract the note
and a small jagged lump
wrapped in Kleenex.

In its place I leave a large silver coin
bearing the bust of Susan B. Anthony.
I know that Mr. Lincoln or even Mr. Hamilton
are popular currency under other pillows.

In my daughter's wobbly manuscript
the instructions are clear:
Please take care of my tooth
brush it every day.

I tuck the tissue and the note
in the bottom drawer
of my jewelry box and wonder
about the exchange—

trust that is absolute
for a dollar,
an assurance I cannot give
even 175 years after Seneca Falls.

She deposits the coin with postcards
and feathers in a glossy foiled cigar box
under her bed—
her currency of hope.

The Sleep of Warriors

Don't go far away, he tells me,
as we stand in the driveway in the dark.
There are monsters and fires.

I want to tell him I know,
that I will slay the dragons,
quench the flames.

Instead, I tell him *Sleep tight,*
his forecast eclipsed by
the adult exchange of hugs and dishes.

At three, he doesn't know the beasts
that batter my nights, but trusts
in something stronger than dreams.

Tired now from downing fiendish brutes,
he nestles in my daughter's arms
and sleeps the sleep of warriors.

I fold into my car
back into the dark and
drive down the mountain.

The highway reaches up and pulls me.
The moon, like fire, rises
over the trees.

Above, Orion leans,
his belt burnishing the skyline,
his sword poised for slaying dragons.

Incongruence

I thought the sky had come unzipped.
Blackness poured down
like dark syrup. But no!
It was only a preening of crows perched
on a mossy arm of the oak
outside my window,

and the endangered species
I thought I'd found
turned out to be
a lost glove
hanging pink and soggy
from the juniper.

I wanted to be right
the night we argued about
something neither of us remembers,
rain pelting the roof,
leaves plastering black
windows I imagined as portals
through which I might disappear,

the irritating tic of time
I mistook for pardon.

Then the warmth of your leg
drooped over mine
while you pretended to be asleep,

and what I thought was silence
was the softness of your earlobe on my cheek.

The Weight of Words

For Christmas my son gave me a pencil—
        made in Taiwan of copper and brass
        that will, apparently, change patina
        with the oil from my fingers.
A thin brochure promises each product is made
        by scorching heat of 1,000 degrees and that
        every pencil is unique.
Fashioned like a shallow drawer, the box it came in
has printed on the lid in lowercase gold letters:
        the weight of words.

How much do my words weigh?

My son, almost 40, carries handfuls of them
        tucked in the creases and folds of his life—
        jangling like cheap chatter or
        weighing down his pockets
        like stones from the river.

My words have bought him
        clemency for poor judgment, blessings,
        and vows to see him through
        the next heartache.

How can we measure their weight?

The human heart, no bigger than a clenched fist,
weighs about 11 ounces.
        How many words does it take to fill one?
        To break one?

Morning with Onion

My husband lifts the knife.
Razor sharp, he insists,
flicks his thumb over the blade.

On the counter the onion
waits—its fawny shell
unfurling, patient as a stone.

He cuts it in half
pole to pole,
lops off the dry, twisted top

and slices the bottom,
careful to leave the stem
intact.

He peels away crisp umber skin,
reminds me, *Onions are cheap,*
tosses a few layers in the compost.

Belly down on the cutting board
the onions tumble
in perfect cubes.

He dabs the tear in my eye,
Propanethial oxide, explains this
scientist chef and tells me

these pearly gems,
craved by Jews in exile,
lavished Olympians with their juices

and gave Ramses IV vision
in the afterlife.
7,000 years of cultivation,

and finally, this morning,
on the counter, he offers up
the omelet.

The Sound of Sleep

Your tufted breaths
the silence of your skin
sheets swished by
your dreaming limbs
restless in so much love
a quiet undertow
pulls us into
each our private darkness
where we listen to the sound
night makes when it falls.

Forgetting

The drawer holds
      nothing.
In it I have left space
      for all I do not know
and what I will not keep.

Fugitive fragrances
      of old linens,
my mother's lingerie linger
      in the spaciousness of memory.

    Was she happy?
Did she really believe in God?
    Did she miss her mother
who she found Plath-like dead?

      Questions become the
      slow sediment of forgetting.

From the house, I watch
      the moon's milk
pour over the field.
      The barred owl calls from the wood,
wind tugs gently at the spruce.

    Do owls mate for life?
How old is the oldest tree?
    And the moon, how does she keep the waves
from pocketing the shoreline?

      Questions I won't bother to answer.
      They take up so little space in the wondering.

My mother said she was tired of requiems,
        flags at half-mast.
She chose to forget
        and planted 1,000 bulbs
that bloomed
        yellow
year after year
        she watched twilight
collect in the pines.
        I loved her for her forgetting.

Photo of My Parents in Their Kitchen

Behind them cups and plates
lined precisely on pine shelves—
her grandmother's china,

his commemorative silver tray,
the glass carafe
decanting years

from the tumble of rocks
that became home on twelve acres
of boggy New England sod.

Her hand reaches for
his freshly shaven chin—
her promise to have and to hold,

for better or worse.
His eyes smile at her through
steam swirled from freshly brewed coffee—

like an old love, no, a new love,
that rests between
the inhale and exhale

of children grown, dogs buried
beneath trees he salvaged,
stone walls slumped between beds of thistle and lily.

Half-eaten toast lies crusty, cold
on the breakfast plate
he has abandoned for her touch.

I'd like to believe this moment
lingers in his forgetting, in
her shortness of breath,

and that on that day
of that year,
whenever it was,

he rose to tend his trees
and she to spread the last load of mulch
on the beds before winter.

What She Carried

My mother hoisted the wicker picnic basket
from the station wagon onto her hip.

She must have told us not to ask questions
and to be quiet before she pushed the steel bar

on the door of the *facility*—what she called it
to her friends. To us, it was the *hospital*.

I walked by her side, my sisters behind us,
holding hands. Our pressed shirt-waist dresses

whispered in the dead air. My father stood waiting,
diminutive in his Harris Tweed, crisp

white shirt, bow tie balanced on his Adam's apple.
In the garden my mother unpacked sandwiches,

potato salad, maybe peaches? We were careful
to eat slowly. Any conversation long forgotten.

There were more visits, maybe one or two,
and later drives to the therapist, in the rain,

just my father and me, along for the company
to keep him engaged, and not *lost in his head.*

In between, there were months, years
of happily-ever-after: parties, friends, croquet,

travel, and always his darknesses
lit by my mother's bon-vivance and grace

that sheltered his gloom—her perfect meals,
gardens of envy, things carefully buttoned up—

and all the while—she carried his silence, her secret—
on her stiff upper lip.

Peaches and Ghosts

The rickety wooden stand groans under the weight
of tomatoes bursting at fleshy folds, soft
and smelling slightly of mold, zucchini
stacked like small torpedoes on broken crates.
My mother hastily greets a friend,
inspects peaches from the South, and peers
inside the bonnets of the corn. She tears
husks, salvaged from the dry rattle of summer's end.
Picked this morning, Tony says and bags
the peaches, beets, red-wrinkled greens
drooping in the humid air. She takes her bounty,
slips behind the wheel and navigates
through fog drifted on the lane
and, as though planned, she passes through my dream.

We are ghost daughters

gathering sea roses and heather
for the funeral pyre.

We have come from your bedside,
left you, statuary: bedclothes tucked
under your chin, face up, dead.

Fog spills on pale dunes
slumped over the beach. We step
into the night, wet sand cradles our steps.

The sky opens up to make room
for you among the stars,
your reflection makes a path

where we stack beach stones.
The cairn casts a shadow in your light—
honoring sister, brother, father, stone by stone.

Have you found us here
in the hush where water curls over
stones deaf to our grief and

clouds feather the horizon?
The moon takes back the water.
I have lost count

of who is living
and who is dead.

A Vacancy

It begins with birdsong, *for now it does*—
The tangled trill of the goldfinch rises—

> The mangled truth of numbers rise
> 2.9 billion fewer birds today.

A lone loon yodels her lament today,
Flute of thrush, drum of flicker, silenced.

> The thrush and drum of science silenced.
> Just three degrees will push our avian friends

From the shores and woods we walk with friends.
The night birds that glide the glassy lake,

> The dawn-catchers pulling night from the lake—
> Whistle and trill fade into vacancy.

The day opens into vacancy.
It begins with birdsong, *until it doesn't.*

darkening

jasmine sweet
summer days
empty
into hollows.

the pause, heavy
with rose and lavender
carries
the mower's last whir
cicadas' drifting thrum.

rain
on hot asphalt
steam rising
to our nostrils.

poplars bend
with the racket of crow and jay
the stealth of warblers
crinkling leaves—

slow summer days
darken rivers
guzzling
the Pleiades.

each day
shorter than the last.
who am I to have
loved this season?

Sunset on the Edisto River

after Lola Haskins

Look! The marsh has eaten fire
and the river has given her gleam back
to the rushes—
bronzed rapiers so still
even the great egret whispers her
way home.

Waking

I wake beside you
   bedclothes rustle like
the papery sound
       of retreating shore birds

your breath
   steady from slow
dreams
   gives pace to my rising.

outside
   waves pummel
       a low tideline

spectral
steam from my tea
      lifts into

morning fog drifts
as the smell of sleep
      holds you.

When you wake
 soon enough
      day pauses

 on the updraft
      a hundred wings
      oaring their way

across the horizon
 you turn
         and I am caught

short by the density
 of love
         your face creased

like wet sand
 the sea of your eyes
             blue.

Gladiolas

My daughter called them gladiators
when she was three and just about
as tall as the volunteer spears
in my garden masquerading
as the lilies I purposely planted.

In my poem she is three, then five,
her tiny hands clad in Wonder Woman
gardening gloves.
Side-by-side we work
digging, planting—
but in truth she never liked to garden.
Instead, she inhabited the lives
of travel agents, pop-stars, maître-d's.
Our silverware drawers burst with
monopoly money, ledgers and menus,
plans for extravagant events
with the rich and famous.

A young mom, I read
Women Who Run With the Wolves,
Our Bodies Ourselves, weeded
the invasives and evils
of pop-culture. How was I so sure
that *Charlotte's Web* would better prepare her
for the world than *The Babysitters' Club?*

Yesterday as I was pruning roses & spreading
the last of the mulch she called to ask
if I would check her resume,
pick up the boys from school.
She wondered if I had zinnias
to spare and how much garlic
to add to French onion soup.

Sometimes I wonder if I confused
the gladiolas with the gladiator—
she who is vanquishing her own beasts
certain, as she is,
that perfection is possible.

I am rewriting this poem and calling it
Gladiator.

Pomme

You are cider in the round
perfume that lingers
only as long as the nose inquires
after the first onomatopoetic bite
into your blushing shoulder.
You are autumn
dimpled and imperfect
as the summer days that
brought your flower to fruit.

Mums

At Ace Hardware
the mums are out,
buds like tiny fists clenched
and green. Tinges of bronze
and garnet peek between
cloven leaves.

In a week
they are a fiesta flouncing
where fall gardeners
search to fill the vacancies
left by campanula and lily.

These mums are loud,
annunciations that shout
from gardens and porches
mocking winter's impending grey.

Half a country away
my mother's mums—
Sheffield Pinks and Clara Curtis
are quieter, they sprawl

and curtsy over
tumbled stone walls
reluctant to give in to
early darkness of cold
New England winters.

Among the ragweed, and goldenrod,
mums complete her story—hands
plunged in rich black soil

curled around root-balls
tenderly nestled amid pastures
of fescue and sedge bent in
the late September sun.

Nothing to a Mountain

for my forever friends, Deb and Marty

I drive into October,
stopping in the village of Quechee
to meet friends I have not seen
since high school.
Over coffee, I feel New England
like an old ache—
chilling, familiar.

We drive on across New Hampshire,
miles of biscuit-colored fields
stretch out before the mountains—
scarlet, vermillion, amber
splashed against a pewter sky.
The road unfolds into the hills along
the Winooski River.

In Kezar Falls rusted reapers
stand like giant grasshoppers
in untended pastures and children
walk to school.
Marty greets us, pulls us
into her life on the farm—
feeding chickens and
two roan horses.

We gather eggs, harvest lettuce
before frost. We dig root vegetables—
mud-clad carrots and beets
that have waited all summer
in the rich Maine soil.

Daylight slips away. Our quiet talk
lifts into hay in the rafters overhead.
We have come a long way. The night is patient.
Fifty years is nothing to a mountain.

About the Author

Alida Woods is one of those Damn Yankees with strong New England roots who has found her home in Asheville, North Carolina for 50 years. A life-long educator, she can be found in or on most any body of water, in her garden, or on adventures with her husband and their dog or her three grandsons.

Her poetry has appeared in *The Amsterdam Quarterly, The Great Smokies Review, Artemis, Smokey Blue Literary Arts Magazine, Front Porch,* and *Litmosphere.* Her chapbook, *Disturbing Borders,* was published by Finishing Line Press in 2018.

She wishes to thank The Great Smokies Writing Project, Poeanon (you know who you are), Charlotte Lit, and her mentors, Lola Haskins and Eric Nelson. Love and thanks to Mollie and Geordie for their generous editing. Alida's family and friends are her grace notes every day.

www.ingramcontent.com/pod-product-compliance
Lightning Source LLC
Chambersburg PA
CBHW030916170426
43193CB00009BA/871